Author:
Brian Williams studied English before teaching in both primary and secondary education. He worked for *Encyclopaedia Britannica* for several years as Editor of *Children's Britannica* and is now a full-time writer.

Artist:
David Antram was born in Brighton, England, in 1958. He studied at Eastbourne College of Art and then worked in advertising for fifteen years before becoming a full-time artist. He has illustrated many children's nonfiction books.

Series creator:
David Salariya

Editor:
Michael Ford

First edition for North America (including Canada and Mexico), the Philippines, and Puerto Rico, published in 2006 by Barron's Educational Series, Inc.

© The Salariya Book Company Ltd MMIV

First published in Great Britain in 2004 by Book House, an imprint of
The Salariya Book Company Ltd
25 Marlborough Place, Brighton BN1 1UB

Please visit the Salariya Book Company at:
www.salariya.com

All inquiries should be addressed to:
Barron's Educational Series, Inc.
250 Wireless Boulevard
Hauppauge, New York 11788
www.barronseduc.com

Library of Congress Control Number: 2005937377

ISBN-13: 978-0-7641-3488-3
ISBN-10: 0-7641-3488-4

Printed and bound in China

Printed on paper from sustainable forests.

Bell
and the science
of the telephone

Written by
Brian Williams

Illustrated by
David Antram

The Explosion Zone

BARRON'S

Contents

Introduction

Can you think of a world without telephones? Not being able to call home to say you'll be late, no text messages, no long chats with friends? The telephone changed the way we live and work.

Alexander Graham Bell is remembered as the "telephone man." The idea was quite simple. Change sounds into electrical signals, send them along a wire, and change them back to sounds again. Other inventors had done this, but Bell was the first to turn the sound into spoken words rather than buzzes and clicks. Bell knew a lot about sound because he was an expert in speech and hearing. The telephone (named from Greek words meaning "far speaker") made him rich, but he still went on inventing. He wanted to help people communicate. Another great inventor, Thomas Edison, said Bell had "brought the human family closer in touch."

Sounds and silence

Alexander Bell (he added the "Graham" later) was born on March 3, 1847, in Edinburgh, Scotland. His father, Alexander Melville Bell, taught students elocution, or how to speak correctly. His mother, Eliza, was a painter who was deaf. At the time when "Aleck" was growing up with his brothers Melville and Ted, people who needed to send a message quickly used the electric telegraph. But the telegraph sent only coded clicks. No one had ever heard the human voice recorded or sent long distance through wires.

I wonder how the sound of the leaves reaches my ears?

Here's the science

Sound waves

*High frequency
(ripples close together)*

*Low frequency
(ripples spread apart)*

Sounds are produced when objects vibrate or move rapidly back and forth. The number of times an object vibrates in a given period of time is called its frequency. Sounds are able to travel through the air as waves. The greater the frequency of a sound wave, the higher the pitch.

WHAT MAKES NOISE?
Aleck liked music and played tunes on anything. He wondered why a comb and paper made a noise when you blew on them. Why did leaves rustle in the wind?

Try it yourself

SOUND RULES. Hold down the short end of a ruler on the edge of a table. Now twang the end that hangs over. BOIING! As the ruler vibrates up and down, it disturbs the air, and makes a sound. No air means no sound. This experiment would not work in space, because there is no air in space!

No star student

Young Aleck didn't go to school until he was ten years old. Instead he read books, went bird-watching, and kept pet animals.

"My dream was to become a musician," Bell once said. At the Royal High School, Aleck was an average student, but he enjoyed learning math. Teachers thought his brother "Melly" was much more clever. But Aleck spent time helping his father. Mr. Bell had worked out a way of writing down sounds to teach deaf children how to speak, called "Visual Speech."

Aleck left school at 14 and spent a year with his grandfather in London. London was a very busy city. It was easy to get knocked over by messengers dashing along the streets from one office to another. Grandfather Bell also took Aleck to meet Professor Charles Wheatstone, the inventor of Britain's first electric telegraph.

TALKING HEAD. The Bell boys built a "talking machine" out of wood, rubber, and sheep's bones. They got it to say "Mama" when they blew into its mouth!

Here's the science

Vocal chords

Vocal chords

To talk, we use our tongue and vocal cords. As air is breathed out of our lungs, it passes through the vocal chords, causing elastic flaps to vibrate like stretched rubber bands, making sounds.

Everyone's in such a rush these days. The streets aren't safe!

TELEGRAPH TAPPING. The telegraph sent urgent messages over long distances by using electrical signals. A tap on the telegraph key opened and closed an electrical circuit, sending clicking sounds along the telegraph wire. Words tapped in coded clicks were heard and decoded at the other end of the wire.

A telegraph machine

9

The young teacher

A t 15, Aleck got his first job, as a teacher in Scotland. He also started to show people how "Visual Speech" worked. In 1866, he made up his mind to leave home and went south to England, taking a teaching job there. He was growing more and more curious about new ways to communicate. With a friend, he rigged up a telegraph wire to send messages between their rooms. Bell already knew a lot about sound; he had tried experiments with drumskins and tuning forks, to find new ways to teach deaf people. Now, by reading books, he found out more about electricity and how batteries, circuits, and electromagnets worked.

Aleck was full of life and energy. But then two terrible blows struck his family. In 1867, his younger brother Ted died of tuberculosis, and three years later his older brother Melly died from the same lung disease. Aleck's life changed from then on.

Say: "biscuit!"

TALKING TERRIER. Aleck tried teaching a dog to speak. He got his terrier to growl the vowel sounds: "ow ah ooh ga ma ma." It sounded like "How are you, Grand-mama?"

This takes too long – there's got to be a better way!

Here's the science

Morse code

Morse code was invented by Samuel Morse of the United States. It uses dots and dashes to write down long and short sounds. Each alphabet letter has its own dot-dash code, so words can be spelled out. Telegraph messages were sent in Morse code, with words spelled out by long or short "clicks."

Bell's name in Morse code.

B – · · ·
E ·
L · – · ·
L · – · ·

Try it yourself

A string phone

Metal can

1) With parental supervision, make a small hole in the bottom of two empty metal cans, using a hammer and nail.
2) Push the string through the holes, and knot the ends so the string won't pull through.
3) Hold one can each. Make sure the string is pulled tight.
4) Speak into one can. Your friend will hear your voice by holding the other can to his ear.

Keep string tight

HOW IT WORKS

The can captures the sounds of the speaker and vibrates, which in turn causes the string to vibrate. These vibrations travel along the string to the other can causing that can to vibrate, and finally the listener to hear the speaker's voice.

11

A new world

After their sons died, Mr. and Mrs. Bell left Britain for Canada, taking Aleck with them. They settled in Ontario, but Aleck got a job in America, at the School for the Deaf in Boston. He was a wonderful teacher to the children and encouraged them to make any noises they could, just to feel the sounds.

In 1872, a great fire broke out in Boston. A new electric fire alarm called out the firefighters, but many buildings burned. Bell also met Mabel Hubbard. She was 15 and had been deaf since the age of 5. Her father, Gardiner Hubbard, was a rich lawyer, interested in new inventions. He and Bell talked about experiments with tuning forks that vibrated when electric current flowed through a circuit. A "harmonic telegraph" using this idea might help deaf people.

Here's the science

Tuning fork

Vibrating outwards

Vibrating inwards

A tuning fork has two metal prongs. Striking the tuning fork with a rubber mallet causes it to vibrate. By placing the tuning fork in a bowl of water, waves can be seen. Many musicians use tuning forks to tune their instruments.

If only they could have been here sooner...

Try it yourself

MAKE A SPEAKING TUBE. Find a long piece of plastic tube. Tape a plastic funnel to each end. Give one end to a friend. Put the funnel to your ear and you can hear your friend whisper from the next room. Why? Once inside the tube, sound waves have to travel down it because they can't escape into the air.

Warning! Don't shout! You might damage your hearing.

Twanging springs!

y 1873, Bell was a professor at Boston University, working on the "harmonic telegraph" in his spare time. Charles Williams was the owner of an electrical workshop who knew almost everything that had been discovered about electricity. He told Bell that Thomas Watson would make a good assistant if he needed one.

Bell's work with tuning forks gave him the idea for a telegraph that could send 12 messages at once, maybe more, by using different "musical" sounds. In June 1875, Bell and Watson were testing wired-up equipment, each in their own room. A metal spring got stuck and Watson plucked it, to make it vibrate properly. An excited Bell ran in from next door. "What did you do just then?" he shouted. Through the wire, he had heard a faint sound – a twanging spring.

Twang!

14

KEEP AT IT. Joseph Henry (1797–1878) was America's most famous electrical scientist. He encouraged Bell to keep going with his experiments.

Here's the science

Twanging spring

Magnetized strip

Stronger current — Circuit — Weaker current

A magnetized metal strip put near a wire coil makes a small electric current in the wire. If the strip vibrates, the current "flickers," first weaker then stronger. Watson's twanging spring had made a tiny electric current. It flowed along the wire into Bell's room and made a "twang" there too.

SPOOKY NAME. A thin skin (like a drumskin) vibrates at the slightest touch. In 1875, Bell and Watson made this "gallows frame" transmitter (right) with an electromagnet (a coil and magnet) and a thin skin (a diaphragm). The skin vibrated, making sounds that the electromagnet turned into tiny electric signals.

Battery

Electromagnet

Diaphragm

The "gallows frame" transmitter

Mr. Watson!

Bell and Watson could now send sounds, like hisses and clicks, through wires, but not proper words yet. They kept trying new ways to make the sounds clearer. On March 9, 1876, Watson talked into the mouthpiece of their latest "telephone." What came out was still "a confused muttering sound."

Bell made some changes to his plans and Watson put together the new apparatus. Under the mouthpiece was a diaphragm, fixed to a platinum needle. The needle touched the surface of a dish filled with water and sulfuric acid.

The next day, March 10, 1876, the two men were working in different rooms, linked by wires. Bell said: "Mr. Watson, come here, I want you!" and Mr. Watson came running in. The telephone worked!

Here's the science

Variable current

This is what Bell's drawing looked like. His voice made the diaphragm vibrate. The movements went through the needle and set up changes in the electrical resistance of the liquid. This sent an electric current (weak and strong by turns) flowing to the receiver, where a vibrating reed reproduced the voice sounds.

Diaphragm

Needle

Liquid

Receiver

The Bell patent

AMAZING SOUNDS. Bell took out a patent for his telephone on March 3, 1876, a week before he made it work. By May, he had shown it to several professors. They were amazed by the "sounds…heard by all who listened into the tube."

You called, Aleck!

Talking to anyone

In June 1876 Bell showed off his telephone at the Centennial Exposition in Philadelphia, an exhibition to celebrate 100 years of the United States. Hearing someone's voice through a wire was a startling way to mark the event. People could hardly believe their ears! By October, Bell had tested his telephone over a 3-mile (5-km) line, and in May 1877 a burglar alarm company began putting the first phones into customers' homes.

In July that year, Bell and Mabel Hubbard were married. They went to Europe on their honeymoon and to Britain, where Bell showed his phone to Queen Victoria. He tried out improvements, adding cone-shapes for the mouthpiece and earpiece. People with poor hearing used a cone-like "ear trumpet" to aid them, because a cone's funnel-shape helps to trap sound.

A ROYAL AUDIENCE. While on his honeymoon in Britain, Bell showed his telephone to Queen Victoria (opposite). She was very impressed with the new invention. She wanted to connect all her different castles by telephone!

My God, it talks!

HAMLET ON THE PHONE. At the Centennial Exposition, Bell demonstrated his new telephone to Emperor Dom Pedro II of Brazil. Bell read one of Hamlet's speeches from Shakespeare's play to the emperor, who was astounded.

Here's the science

Catching the sound

Megaphone

Sound waves

Ear trumpet

The cone shape of a megaphone or bullhorn stops sound waves from spreading out too quickly so they travel further. The cone of an ear trumpet (an old-fashioned hearing aid) acts like a net to catch sound waves and funnel the sound to the ear.

Which end do I speak into?

Try it yourself

1) To make a megaphone, fold a square sheet of paper into a triangle, as shown.

2) Roll the paper triangle into a cone shape. Stick the edges together with tape.

3) Cut off the narrow end of the cone, to make a mouthpiece. Call to a friend. Is your voice louder?

Warning!
Ask an adult to help you use the pair of scissors.

19

Wires everywhere!

Bell set up his own telephone company in 1877. But he had a rival, the American Elisha Gray, who had patented his telephone just hours after Bell.

News of the telephone spread fast. One hundred were sold in 1877. Within 18 months, there were 1,700 in use. At first, each phone was wired directly to another one, but in 1878 the first "telephone exchange" opened in Connecticut. The first "operators" to "exchange" or "switch" calls between phone lines were Emma and Stella Nutt. Their first phone book had 50 names, but no numbers. London had its first exchange in 1879 – with only eight phones connected to it!

North America had more than 130,000 phones by 1881. A delighted Bell saw city streets festooned with telephone wires, strung from poles. Other companies set up telephone services too, sending workers racing around to string up wires. Some customers complained that rival wires had cut off their phone calls!

Bell tried not to let business, or his family of two daughters, take his mind off inventing. In 1882 he invented a machine for recording sounds. He called it the graphophone – an improvement on Edison's phonograph.

Bell might not have submitted his patent before Elisha Gray without the help of Lewis Latimer (right). Latimer worked through the night to draw the patent design. He later worked with Thomas Edison inventing filaments, the glowing wires inside light bulbs.

Lewis Latimer

Here's the science

How a modern exchange works

The first telephone exchanges needed people to plug wires in and out of switchboards. Today, calls are sent digitally. A multiplexer changes the sound signals into electronic digital signals, and a de-multiplexer turns them back into sounds again. Thousands of calls whizz along every second.

Sound signal

Line multiplexer

Coded digital signals

De-multiplexer

SOUNDS BETTER. With the prize money he won for his telephone invention, Bell set up a research laboratory where he and his team invented the graphophone. It recorded sounds onto a spinning wax-covered drum. To play back, a stylus (needle) retraced the marks on the wax.

Stylus

Wax

Bell's graphophone

Look, the whole city's connected!

Number, please

Bell had to spend time and money in the law courts to settle a patent dispute with Elisha Gray. Gray had worked on the "liquid transmitter" idea before Bell, but in the end, Bell won the case.

Americans liked the telephone. It was the fastest way to keep in touch and do business: a letter took days to cross the country by steam train and horse. By 1880, there were 30,000 phones in the United States. Four years later, the first long-distance phone call was made, between Boston and New York. But there were problems. Calls could "jump" from one wire to another, and the new electric lights affected some people's phones. A funeral director named Almon Strowger was so annoyed when a rival firm kept getting his calls that in 1890 he invented an automatic switchboard. He built the wiring inside a wooden coffin!

GET OFF THE LINE! The writer Mark Twain (left) was one of the first phone-owners. He was furious when his calls got cut off or he heard someone else's voice on the line!

Carbon microphone

Carbon granules

Sound waves

Electric current to receiver

Diaphragm

Thomas Edison put a carbon microphone in his phone. The diaphragm inside vibrated as he spoke, making tiny carbon granules jump about. The carbon's electrical resistance changed, causing a changing electrical current along the phone wire. This made speech sound more lifelike.

A BELL PHONE of the 1880s looked like the diagram below. Inside the rubber case was an electromagnet. Speaking made a diaphragm vibrate, which set up an electrical signal in the coil. The signal went along wires to the receiver. Here it set up vibrations in another diaphragm and reproduced the words spoken.

ELECTRICAL WHIZZ. Edison (right) invented the carbon microphone in 1877 and the phonograph, his recording machine, in 1878. Although Edison sold his telephone to Bell's rival, Western Union, he and Bell still became friends.

wire coil

Wires connected to coil

Soft iron diaphragm

Mouthpiece

bar magnet

rubber casing

The telephone age

The telephone was improving all the time. New phones had both transmitter and receiver in one handset. Copper wires proved much better than the iron wiring first used (copper is a better electrical conductor). Underground cables meant fewer wires strung across streets. Signal-boosting made really long-distance calls possible – in 1892 Bell made the first call from New York to Chicago. By 1907 there were over six million phones in America. A new phone with direct-dial numbers offered a privacy service. Before that, all calls went through an operator, who could listen in.

As the telephone became part of everyday life, Bell kept busy with new ideas and interests, such as America's National Geographical Society and his work to help deaf people, such as Helen Keller (see page 25).

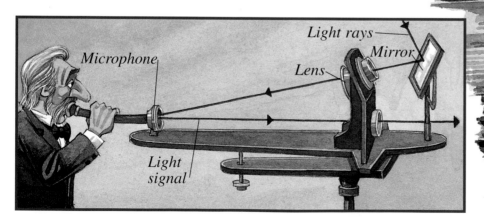

THE "PHOTOPHONE." One of Bell's new ideas was to try and send the human voice using light instead of wires. Bell's photophone worked by projecting the voice through an instrument toward a mirror. Vibrations caused in the mirror made light reflect differently and these fluctuating light signals could be turned back into sound by a light receiver some distance away.

Fiber optics

Transmitter

Signals travel as coded pulses

Receiver

Fiber optic cable in sheath

Modern fiber optics work as light rays and are reflected off the inside of a hair-thin glass or plastic tube. The light zigzags along inside. Bundles of fibers in a cable carry huge amounts of coded signals, at amazing speed. A fiber optic cable can carry thousands more telephone calls than an old-fashioned metal wire.

Hello, Chicago, can you hear me?

A REMARKABLE PERSON. Helen Keller (1889–1968) was left deaf and blind after an illness at the age of 19 months. Bell suggested Helen visit a teacher from Boston, Anne Sullivan. She taught Helen to communicate using "hand-spelling" and the Braille "raised dot" alphabet. Bell and Helen became good friends.

Never still

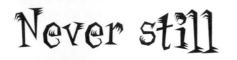

The Bell summer home was at *Beinn Bhreagh*, or "beautiful mountain" in Gaelic, an ancient language used in Ireland and Scotland. The big house in Nova Scotia became a place for fun and research for the Bell family. Mabel Bell gave up trying to stop her husband from working. He was too full of ideas, many of which he liked to try out on his family – such as odd-shaped kites and pyramid-shaped engineering structures. Although he once said "I somehow or other appear to be more interested in things than people," he loved his family and playing with his nine grandchildren. He gave money away generously to fund laboratories, prizes, scholarships, and schools for the deaf.

An early dial telephone

DIAL A NUMBER. While Bell busied himself with his many interests, the phone business kept on the move too. Small companies sold new phones, like this early dial phone (above).

Both Bell and his wife were fascinated by flight (the Bell company later built planes and helicopters). Bell also took an interest in hydrofoil craft for high-speed water travel.

You see! I told you it would fly!

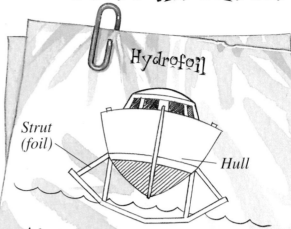

Hydrofoil

Strut (foil)

Hull

A hydrofoil rests on wing-like struts called foils. The foils lift the boat clear of the water as it gains speed, so that the hull "flies" above the surface. Because it meets less water resistance or friction, a hydrofoil skims over the water faster than an ordinary craft.

WATER SKIMMER. Bell called his hydrofoil boats "hydro-dromes." In 1918, his HD-4 craft set a hydrofoil world speed record of 71 miles per hour (114 kph) – a record not broken until 1963.

Communications revolutionary

Bell died on August 2, 1922, at the age of 75, honored as the inventor who made "calling someone" part of everyday life. At the start of his funeral, every phone in North America was silent for one minute. In just a few years, Bell saw his telephone change the way people kept in touch and did business. Five years after Bell died, the first telephone call across the Atlantic Ocean was made, by cable.

Since Bell's time, telephone technology has moved on rapidly. Thanks to fiber optics, computer modems, cell phones, and communications satellites, a phone lets us talk, text, or send information from almost any spot on the planet. Bell expected life to go on changing. "Education is a lifelong affair," he told a young reporter the year before his death.

Satellite links

Cell phone

Transceiver

Nearest station

Satellite in space

Cell phones send signals by radio waves. The signals are picked up by a mast antenna covering an area known as a cell. Each cell's transceiver (transmitter and receiver) station is linked to the main phone network. Satellites in orbit around the Earth beam phone signals between continents.

Glossary

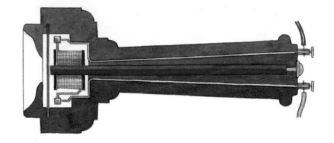

Battery A device containing two substances that react chemically to produce electricity.

Carbon A common natural material – coal, charcoal and diamonds are forms of carbon.

Circuit The complete path taken by an electrical current along a suitable conductor.

Code A system for changing one kind of information (such as sounds) into another (such as electrical signals).

Conductor A substance that allows electricity to flow through it easily.

Current The flow of electrons along a conductor, such as a wire.

Diaphragm A flexible layer, like a skin, which vibrates in air and in a microphone that can send and receive sound waves.

Digital switching A way of changing continuous electrical current into a sequence of "0" and "1" ("on-off") electrical signals.

Electromagnet A magnet which works only when a current passes through a coil of wire wrapped around an iron core.

Elocution The study of speech and teaching people to speak properly.

Fiber optics The method of sending light-signals at very high speed through thin glass or plastic tubes bundled together.

Frequency The number of (sound) waves produced within a given period of time. The frequency of a sound wave determines its pitch. The greater the frequency of a sound wave, the higher the pitch.

Harmonic telegraph A device in which an electric current carries notes or sounds.

Magnetism The invisible force that attracts some metals and is given out by an electric current as well as by some substances.

Modem A device that links a computer to the phone network in the internet.

Patent An inventor's description of a new invention, filed at a patent office so that no other inventor can copy the same invention.

Platinum A rare and expensive metal that is very resistant to corrosion.

Radio A form of radiation, used to send sounds through the air without wires.

Resistance The amount of opposition a material has to the flow of electric current through it.

Satellite A spacecraft held in orbit around a planet by gravity.

Sound Vibrations in the air which we, and animals, sense with our ears and hear with our brains.

Technology Science put to practical use, using systems and equipment made by inventors.

Telegraph A communications system for message-sending, invented in an electrical form in the 1830s (earlier systems used moving flags, levers, or lights).

Tuning fork A two-pronged metal fork used by musicians to sound a note.

Variable current An electric current that changes strength, and so can produce different effects in a linked apparatus.

Vibrations Fast movements, up and down or from side to side.

Index

To read more about the fascinating life of Alexander Graham Bell and the legacy of his research, try these internet links:

bell.uccb.ns.ca
www.iath.virginia.edu/albell/homepage.html
www.agbell.org
DON'T FORGET TO ASK PERMISSION AT HOME OR IN SCHOOL BEFORE USING THE INTERNET.